Original title:
Tendrils of Thought

Copyright © 2025 Creative Arts Management OÜ
All rights reserved.

Author: Giselle Montgomery
ISBN HARDBACK: 978-1-80581-746-8
ISBN PAPERBACK: 978-1-80581-273-9
ISBN EBOOK: 978-1-80581-746-8

Stargazing Thoughts in the Dusk

In the twilight, minds do soar,
Chasing dreams on a cosmic floor.
A squirrel's wink, a star's bright jest,
Cosmic giggles, who knows best?

Pondering planets, a dance of tones,
While my cat plots to topple my phones.
Aliens call, or is it just me?
Their laughter echoes, wild and free.

Ideas stretch like spaghetti strands,
Twirling and twiddling through our hands.
A comet sneezed, it's all a show,
What's the punchline? We don't quite know.

Moonbeams tickle, the sky's a clown,
Jupiter winks, the world turns brown.
Cupcakes float, a galaxy parade,
In this chaos, the mind's unmade.

Unraveled Mysteries

In the attic, dust bunnies sway,
Old secrets whisper, then run away.
Socks in a corner, I can't find one,
The puzzle's confusion has just begun.

A cat on a shelf gives me a stare,
As if he knows all that's hidden there.
Keys to my life jingle and jive,
While I'm just trying to stay alive.

The Web of Realization

I spun my dreams on a bright blue day,
But tripped on the strings, oh what a play!
A sandwich, a cat, and a lost shoe too,
Life's a circus; the clowns are you.

My thoughts like spaghetti, all twisted and nice,
A fork at the ready, oh how I entice.
With laughter and folly, I seek the light,
As I dance with my brain in a comical fight.

Knots of Awareness

Life's lessons are tangled, a yarn ball of fun,
I pull at a thread, then it comes undone.
Thoughts slide like ribbon through fingers so loose,
Finding more chaos, yet feeling profuse.

Each pondered idea now pleads for a break,
While my brain does the cha-cha, for goodness' sake!
A dance of enlightenment, laughs float around,
As I trip on my thoughts, I just fall to the ground.

Silken Streams of Insight

A river of giggles flows through my mind,
Where wisdom and folly are perfectly aligned.
I ride on the currents, a silly old boat,
With paddles of laughter, I happily float.

Insights like bubbles pop up in the air,
I chase them and giggle—oh, life isn't fair!
But who needs the answers when joy is the prize?
I'll dance through the questions, with stars in my eyes.

Frayed Edges of Contemplation

In the corner of my mind,
Thoughts play hide and seek,
One wears socks that don't match,
The other laughs and squeaks.

A sandwich speaks in riddles,
Telling tales of yesteryears,
The mustard's lost its shimmer,
And now it just sheds tears.

Memories dance like marionettes,
On strings made of spaghetti,
They trip over their own feet,
And end up looking petty.

A cloud starts imitating,
A sheep with a funny face,
It drifts into a giggle,
And makes the sun lose pace.

Knotted Paths of Yesterday

Walking down a twisted lane,
Where thoughts get trapped in knots,
I find my key lost in my sock,
And laugh at such silly spots.

An old shoe says it knew me well,
We ventured far and wide,
But now it's lost its left foot's bite,
Just blabbing with its pride.

Dust bunnies in a lively chat,
They gossip 'bout the past,
They claim to know all secrets,
But none of them can last.

A squirrel steals my sandwich near,
And scurries up a tree,
I shout, 'Hey, that's mine, you thief!'
And he just shakes with glee.

Chasing the Echoes of Enchantment

Echoes of laughter ring around,
In the garden of my head,
A duck wears a wizard's hat,
As he dances in the spread.

Butterflies trade their stories,
While sipping on sweet tea,
One claims to be a dragon,
If only you could see.

A flower sings in harmony,
With a beetle on guitar,
Together they compose a tune,
That travels near and far.

I chase the sounds of silence,
But trip over my own feet,
The garden chuckles softly,
As I fall in pure defeat.

Dreamlike Puzzles in Dusk

As twilight flutters in with grace,
My thoughts begin to wander,
A puzzle made of marshmallows,
Leaves me clueless, filled with wonder.

An owl wearing disco pants,
Attempts to find its groove,
With a dance that spins in circles,
It makes the shadows move.

The moon plays peek-a-boo with me,
Trying on a cloak of mist,
While stars trade silly secrets,
In a sparkle they can't resist.

Dreams tiptoe through the evening,
In shoes too big to wear,
I grin at all their antics,
Floating in the twilight air.

The Labyrinth Within

In a maze of tangled dreams,
Socks wander off in teams.
Jellybeans jump in glee,
As cats chase shadows from a tree.

Whispers curl like playful smoke,
While coffee cups begin to poke.
Laughter echoes down the hall,
As secrets trip and tumble, fall.

Thoughts bounce like balls in flight,
Witty nonsense takes to the height.
Ticklish giggles skip along,
Dancing to the mind's own song.

Lost ideas play a game,
Each one tries to stake its claim.
With a wink, they twirl and shout,
Silly notions all about.

Stalks of Curiosity

Little green vines peek about,
As thoughts play hide and seek, no doubt.
Questions sprout like wildflowers,
Blooming brightly for long hours.

Wisps of wonder weave their way,
With giggles that brighten the day.
Insects chat and share their views,
While pondering life's odd shoes.

A curious mind bounces fast,
Chasing shadows, having a blast.
Wandering where the wild things roam,
Creating mischief far from home.

Tickled fancies laugh and rise,
With quirky dreams that improvise.
Through whimsy's fertile ground, we leap,
Harvesting laughter, not too deep.

Woven Echoes of Being

In looms of laughter, threads intertwine,
Weaving tales like sweet sunshine.
Whimsical whispers skip a beat,
As socks escape in a shoe retreat.

Echoes dance with silly flair,
While dreaming minds glide through the air.
Colorful yarns pull tight and tease,
Laughing loudly at life's little cheese.

Spools of whimsy roll around,
Finding joy in the silliness found.
Knots of chaos hold the mirth,
Making giggles burst forth from the earth.

Fanciful stitches craft the day,
While puzzling thoughts mischievously play.
In the tapestry of what we feels,
Joyful echoes are our reels.

Threads of the Mind's Eye

A spool of thoughts spins ever tight,
Creating chaos in morning light.
Imaginations twist and twirl,
Dancing in pajamas, giving a whirl.

Snippets of laughter thread through the air,
Chasing giggles without a care.
Thoughts drift like clouds in a blue sky,
While cereal boats sail pass by.

The silly yarn of life entwines,
Crafting stories with grapevine lines.
Each idea pops like bubblegum,
Splatters of fun, an emergency, dumb!

Woven dreams tumble to the ground,
In a joyful mess, hilariously bound.
With every stitch and every laugh,
Life's grand tapestry made of whimsy's craft.

Foliage of Ideas Unraveled

In the garden of my mind, we play,
Where wild notions sprout every day.
A squirrel stole my best plot twist,
Now he's trying to stage a heist!

Thoughts grow like weeds, oh my luck,
Planted one seed, got a whole truck!
Bouncing around like a rubber ball,
Each crazy idea's a ballad to call.

My head's a jungle, a curious place,
In this tangle, I trip with grace.
Chasing a thought, I lose track of time,
But in this mess, I find my rhyme.

Dancing through branches, I lose my way,
A vine whispers secrets it won't betray.
With giggles and gasps, I seek the prize,
A treasure trove hidden within the skies.

The Nomadic Soul's Reverie

Wanderlust tickles the brain's seams,
Cabins in the clouds and sun-drenched beams.
Packing my thoughts like a colorful kite,
Reality laughed, saying, 'You might!'

Chasing dreams on a cat's fuzzy back,
Wobbly pathways, oh, what a track!
I pirouette on a cinnamon whirl,
Each twirl births a fantastical swirl.

A laughing heart sings to the trees,
"Where's my passport?" it teases the breeze.
I'm a tourist in my own tangled chest,
Each whim a postcard, I send it west.

Bubbles of reason float in the air,
Popping with joy, without a care.
Catch me, dear traveler, if you can,
In this carnival of a whimsical plan.

Inkblots of Wandering Sentiment

A splatter of ink on the page alludes,
To a jester's heart, dancing in moods.
Scraps of ideas take flight in the night,
While my thoughts zigzag without plight.

Masked in mirth, my pen skips a beat,
Creating a chorus of incomplete.
Riding the waves of a quirky thought,
With every inkblot, a story is wrought.

Spilling my secrets like paint on the floor,
Colors collide, then wander out the door.
Was it a dream or a chocolate stain?
Artistry blooms from the oddest of pain.

Laughter escapes from the paper's embrace,
In the chaos of thoughts, I find my place.
With whimsy and giggles, I dance with glee,
A gallery of nonsense, just for me.

Amorphous Currents of Creation

Ideas flow like jellyfish in tide,
Soft and wobbly, they twist and glide.
They bounce around like a dog on a spree,
Chasing its tail, wild and free.

Scribbles and doodles in luminous light,
Each flicker of thought, a playful sight.
A whirlwind of nonsense stirring up fun,
Until the cheese on the toast is done.

Floating thoughts in a cosmic stew,
What if a moonbeam wore a shoe?
The laughter erupts from the quirkiest mix,
Finding joy in the oddest of tricks.

As colors collide, chaos reigns supreme,
In the world of ideas, I live my dream.
Bubbling laughter rides on each wave,
In this ocean of whimsy, I misbehave.

Threads of Intrigue in the Ether

In the corners of my mind, a sock,
It pairs with thoughts that seem to mock.
Flying past on trails of glee,
Chasing whispers, can't catch me!

Ideas twirl like autumn leaves,
Tied together like Joe's worn sleeves.
A feathered hat, a rubber shoe,
Who thinks these dreams could be so few?

Spaghetti strands of past regrets,
Dance with laughter, a need for bets.
Jellybeans scatter in my wake,
What will I eat? What will I bake?

Fuzzy rabbits hop along,
They sing my mind a silly song.
With poky sticks and silly rules,
Life is better with some fools!

Shadows of a Wandering Memory

Memories flicker, a cheeky sprite,
Sipping tea, refusing to bite.
Yesterday's laugh wraps round my waist,
Like a burrito, oh what a taste!

The kitchen clock swings left and right,
Telling tales of late-night fights.
A dance in the cupboard, the cats all cheer,
While grandma's cookies disappear.

Foggy thoughts, a tangled braid,
With popsicle sticks, dreams are made.
Got lost in the cupboard, where's my shoe?
Next to silly hats, and a rubber zoo!

Light bulbs flicker, a game of tag,
Racing shadows in a colored rag.
Confetti dreams and a disco ball,
We laugh out loud, we trip and fall!

Veins of Curiosity

Curiosity's a cheeky friend,
With every question, there's a bend.
What's in there? What's beyond?
A universe of fish and pond!

The cat's in the hat with a squishy grin,
Searching for where the giggles begin.
An octopus plays peek-a-boo,
Holding secrets that we pursue.

Jumping beans tap-dance alone,
While jellyfish make the phone call home.
Why does the toaster always sing?
Oh what fun this madness can bring!

With every thought, a curious nibble,
Like a cat that plays with its scribble.
Questions bounce like bouncy balls,
In a park where no one stalls!

Latticework of Silent Musings

Silent musings weave a thread,
In a garden where garden gnomes tread.
Whispers giggle in clay pots too,
Planning antics for me and you.

A squirrel wears a tiny suit,
Discussions held down by the root.
With mushroom hats and berry stains,
They offer us their food campaigns.

Every shadow has something to say,
Like playful kittens in their play.
A joke shared with a potted fern,
As I sit back, it's my turn!

Oven timers dance with grace,
Tick-tock rumble, join the race.
With a sprinkle of fun and a pinch of glee,
Life's a giggle—come laugh with me!

Whispers in the Attic

Up in the attic, where dust bunnies play,
Thoughts make a ruckus, all night and all day.
A hat wearing glasses, a shoe with a grin,
Chasing the secrets that hide deep within.

A cat on a shelf gives a curious stare,
As ideas skitter, like squirrels in the air.
They doodle and dance, those far-fetched plans,
While the cobwebs giggle, wiggling their strands.

Fragile Threads of Mind

A thought popped up like a bubble of gum,
It floated away, now it's nowhere and numb.
With brainwaves tangled like spaghetti spread,
I'm searching for clarity, lost in my head.

Butterflies laughing, they flit to and fro,
While neurons play tag—what a wild show!
Each tickle of humor, as zany as pie,
Makes sense of the nonsense, oh me, oh my!

Echoes in the Garden

In the garden of giggles, ideas take root,
Where daisies are gossiping, silly and cute.
A carrot wears glasses, a tomato sings low,
As broccoli bows and steals all the show.

The shadows are chuckling, the breezes conspire,
As parsnips share jokes that ignite their own fire.
Thoughts flit like butterflies, spreading their cheer,
While the garden of laughs grows year after year.

Weaving the Unseen

In a weave of absurdity, laughter is spun,
As sunbeams and giggles outshine everyone.
A sock puppet whispers a joke in my ear,
While the spiders are snickering—what a weird sphere!

Stitch by stitch, the fabric of folly,
Creates patterns of joy, all jumbled and jolly.
This tapestry of chuckles, both bright and surreal,
Wraps around my thoughts with a whimsical feel.

Hushed Conversations with the Wind

The breeze plays tricks on my hair,
Whispering jokes that go nowhere.
Squirrels chuckle, trees join in,
A jest so grand, where to begin?

I ask the clouds for a good pun,
They just float by, not even one.
Grass blades giggle, a silent cheer,
As I ramble on, they lend an ear.

I question stars about their fate,
They blink and laugh, 'Don't be late!'
The sun rolls over, catching rays,
Winking at me in bright displays.

With every gust, joy takes its flight,
Nature's uproar, a comedic sight.
I share my secrets with the sky,
In this wild banter, we float high.

Reaching Out to Celestial Musings

I waved to Mars, he waved back slow,
'How's life up here?' 'A cosmic show!'
The Milky Way snickered, 'What a sight!'
'Just don't trip, or miss your flight!'

I pondered Pluto, small but spry,
'Hey, little guy, how do you fly?'
He grinned and said, 'Just take a chance,
And join the stars in this wild dance!'

A comet zoomed by with a grin,
'Catch my tail, let the fun begin!'
I grabbed a nebula for a ride,
Through laughs and spins, we looped and glided.

As I dangle near the moon's big face,
I joked, 'Is this your final place?'
With laughter echoing in space's dome,
I felt the universe calling me home.

Flickering Ember of Imagination

A spark ignites behind my eyes,
Ideas twirl like fireflies.
They dance and prance, a lively crew,
Each one shouting, 'Pick me! Choose me!'

I catch a tale, oh what a thrill,
Stuck in my brain, it won't sit still.
A dragon ducks, then leaps so high,
'Can I take you for a joyride?'

A silly thought sizzles, takes flight,
'Tell me a joke, let's start the night!'
And laughter bubbles, bright and clear,
Each giggle splashing like a cheer.

With every flicker, the stories spin,
A whirlwind of chuckles tucked within.
So gather round, let our minds collide,
In this cozy blaze, let laughter reside.

Captured Whispers between Shadows

In the corner where shadows play,
I hear them gossip the night away.
'There goes the cat, up to her tricks!'
'The light's too bright, but her jump's slick!'

They whisper tales of moons gone shy,
While twinkling stars wink from on high.
A shadow yawned, stretched to the floor,
'Hey, watch it, pal! You'll knock the door!'

The dark chuckled at a lost shoe,
'Was it lost or just seeking a view?'
Shadows huddled, secrets shared,
In this dim glow, no one was scared.

When dawn tiptoes, they bid goodbye,
'We'll meet again whenever you sigh!'
In laughter's echo, they drift away,
A funny show that bids the day.

Rippling Waves of Inspiration

A daydream floats on coffee steam,
While ideas dance, a silly theme.
Thoughts chase each other in playful flight,
Ping-ponging around, oh what a sight!

Bubbles of laughter burst in the air,
Chasing the cat, in a whimsical dare.
Jokes sneak in like whispers on the breeze,
As I ponder my socks, mismatched with ease.

Tickling my brain with playful glee,
Silly musings like ants at a spree.
Frogs in top hats, a curious bunch,
Hopping and skipping, a jolly punch!

So here I sit with a grin on my face,
Riding the waves, embracing the space.
With humor as fuel and joy as a goal,
Crafting these verses from the depths of my soul.

Cascades of Memory beneath the Stars

Under the blanket of a starry night,
Memories twirl like fireflies in flight.
Each one giggles as it flits away,
Recalling the pranks of a long-lost day.

The dog in my dream sings off-key,
A serenade meant just for me.
Grandma's old stories are slippery fish,
Slipping and sliding—oh how they swish!

I reach for a thought but it hums and dances,
Wearing a tutu, taking new chances.
Lost in a whirl of colorful yarn,
Each thread a reminder of when we had fun.

With laughter that echoes in the midnight air,
The past throws its arms wide, without a care.
Stars wink above like they're part of the play,
Guiding my mind in a whimsical way.

Weaving Through the Labyrinth of Spirit

In a maze of giggles, I twirl and spin,
Chasing my worries, I take it on the chin.
Ghosts in the halls wearing mismatched shoes,
A bouncy castle, full of colorful hues.

Thoughts like confetti, a playful storm,
Cacophony of chuckles keeps me warm.
Each corner I turn, there's a joke or a pun,
Like puppies in pajamas, oh what fun!

Wrapped in a riddle, wrapped in a rhyme,
Dancing with shadows, losing all time.
The walls whisper secrets, tickling my ears,
Banishing doubts and childhood fears.

So onward I go, in this fun little chase,
With joy as my compass, I find my place.
The labyrinth twists, but I walk with a grin,
In this tapestry of laughter, I feel alive within!

Touching the Void with Quiet Questions

Quiet questions start to sway,
In the silence, they laugh and play.
What if the moon wore disco lights?
Or penguins had wild karaoke nights?

Doubts flutter like butterflies, so free,
A tickle of whimsy, can't you see?
Scrambled thoughts blurt out on a whim,
Like a teetering cat, they dance on a limb.

Why do socks always vanish in pairs?
Is there a sock thief that laughs at our cares?
Thoughts tumble around like a jester's trick,
Poking their heads out, a cheeky flick.

So I ponder aloud in this vast little void,
With questions that happen to leave me overjoyed.
Each silly notion, a star in my mind,
Whispers of laughter, so sweet and kind.

Twists of Memory

In the attic of my mind, quite a mess,
Old toys are dancing in their Sunday best.
Forgotten squeaks and giggles abound,
A lost sock gets up, twirls around.

I search for my keys, where could they be?
Amongst a parade of the cat and me.
The fridge hums softly, a sweet serenade,
While the leftover pizza tries to evade.

A note from last week just makes me laugh,
'Next week I will train, or at least, take a bath!'
What's this fun game of hide and seek?
Is that my old diary giving a cheeky peek?

Time and again, I lose my mind,
A comical circus of the silliest kind.
Laughter rings out as I open a door,
To half-remembered days and so much more.

The Lattice of Intuition

Jumbled thoughts like a game of ducks,
Waddle along with silly plucks.
My brain's a maze, twisty and neat,
Where ideas bump and shuffle their feet.

A lightbulb moment? Where's the switch?
When boredom strikes, it can be quite a glitch.
I ponder snacks, yet dinner still looms,
Thoughts collide like flowers in bloom.

The whispers of wisdom tickle my ear,
'Tomorrow will be grand, or at least, have beer.'
So I twirl in circles, round and around,
In a lattice of nonsense, joy is found.

Curious creatures in my head roam free,
Naming them all is a funny decree.
Oh, to be lost in a web spun with grace,
Where the laughter connects us in this crazy race.

Ripples in the Cerebral Sea

In a fishbowl mind where the goldfish swim,
Thoughts take a plunge, then do little spins.
Waves of giggles splash as they sway,
Seeking the jellybeans that float away.

A pirate ship sails on a candy wave,
With marshmallow cannons, it's quite brave.
Finding treasures in the brainy tide,
Snacks in the hold—what a joyful ride!

Memories bubble up like fizzy soda,
Navigating currents like a goofy Yoda.
Sharp ideas break like shells on the shore,
While I ponder the last time I danced on the floor.

Each ripple brings laughter, a outburst of fun,
In the vast ocean of thoughts where we run.
So grab your floatie, let's take a dive,
Together we'll swim where the silly vibes thrive.

Silhouettes of Connection

Under the moon's glow, odd shapes take flight,
Dancing shadows on a cool starry night.
Friends of laughter with chuckles galore,
Swaying like branches, who could ask for more?

Mismatched ideas whisper secrets of bliss,
Like cookies and milk, it's a sweet, silly kiss.
A round of high-fives echoes through the air,
Where humor unfurls, without a care.

In this hearty gathering of jests and jives,
Each quirk and each giggle brings the vibes.
We tiptoe around both giggles and glares,
Creating a tapestry that laughs and cares.

So let's paint the night with silly refrains,
Like crayons gone wild on colorful trains.
In the silhouettes of connection we find,
A whimsical canvas, one of a kind.

Threads of Ambivalence in Daylight

In the sun, my brain does play,
Ideas twist and dance away.
One says 'yes', the other 'no',
Like a clown on a tightrope show.

Should I nap or should I snack?
My thoughts swirl like a simple act.
Should I sing or just stay mute?
I trial out each silly route.

Coffee brews, it steals my mind,
It juggles wits as I unwind.
Why does my sock get lost at sea?
It must be plotting against me!

In daylight, thoughts take silly forms,
Like unicorns amidst rainstorms.
Laughing at my tangled haze,
A silly maze in sunlit ways.

Gardens of the Past in Blossoms

In the garden, time does bloom,
Past mistakes are wild perfume.
I tripped on memories like weeds,
While watering my planted seeds.

Old friendships sprout like daisies bright,
Each laugh echoes in the light.
Oh, the one who wore strange hats,
A squirrel in my chat, imagine that!

There's a flower named 'Oops, I Forgot',
Brightly colored, but it's quite a lot.
Petals tell tales of mischief made,
In the sunlight, regrets just fade.

With each bloom, a chuckle grows,
Gardens laughter gently sows.
Past and present swirl in glee,
In this garden, I must be free!

The Spectrum of Sound in Silence

In silence, thoughts begin to hum,
Like bees that buzz, yet they're quite dumb.
An echo sneezes, 'Achoo!' it sounds,
And laughter booms, where stillness bounds.

Whispers tickle like playful sprites,
Soundless giggles fill the nights.
I hear the chairs all start to squeak,
As shadows dance and spirits peek.

Silence wears a noisy crown,
Calls from crickets, up and down.
Yet in this quiet, chaos plays,
The loudest thoughts have no delays.

Lost in soundless music's trance,
I step upon a dreamer's dance.
In silence, humor finds its stride,
A chuckle echoing inside!

Kaleidoscope of Dreams in Motion

In dreams, I soar like socks in flight,
Twist and turn in sheets of night.
One moment I'm a pizza slice,
The next, a cat who thinks it's nice.

With every blink, I change my role,
I'm a taco and it's noon-time stroll.
Dancing llamas lead the way,
In this wacky night ballet.

Colors swirl like ice cream cones,
While my thoughts play in silly tones.
Chasing butterflies on roller skates,
Laughing at the world's odd fates.

In this dream, all seems just right,
Where shadows rave in sheer delight.
Kaleidoscope of chaos, bright,
As whims make merry in the night!

Entangled in Dreams.

In the night, my brain takes flight,
Chasing socks that dance in light.
A fridge that sings, a cat that prances,
Dreams are wild, with silly glances.

I trip on thoughts that twist and twirl,
Jumping jacks with a dizzy whirl.
Nonsense spins like a carousel,
In my head, it's hard to tell.

Where's my shoe? Oh, there it is!
Playing hide and seek, what a fizz!
Giraffes play chess, while dogs just laugh,
In this whimsical, goofy path.

Awake! I shake off these jumbled slips,
As breakfast laughs and bacon skips.
Today's a jest, so come and join,
With all these thoughts, we'll surely conjoin.

Whispers in the Mind's Garden

In my mind, a garden grows,
Where tomato plants wear funny clothes.
Lettuce chuckles, dancing wide,
While carrots joke and take a slide.

A sunflower winks, its petals bright,
Stealing secrets in the bright sunlight.
Bees in tophats swirl around,
Buzzing jokes without a sound.

A cabbage crowned with silly flair,
Offers laughs beyond compare.
In this patch of green delight,
Thoughts can frolic, taking flight.

So skip with me through this strange maze,
Where thoughts bloom wildly in funny ways.
Let's dig deep into laughter's dirt,
And plant some joy beneath the hurt.

Echoes of Unfurling Dreams

In my head, a race begins,
Where thoughts collide like silly twins.
Barrels roll with giggling glee,
Echoing dreams like a bumblebee.

A fish wears glasses, reading lore,
As thoughts bounce back, seeking more.
Painting skies in shades of fun,
Hilarity's chase has just begun.

I whisper secrets to a wall,
And watch it giggle, then enthrall.
Each echo brings a joke anew,
I laugh so hard, am I a fool?

But who's the fool in this grand scheme?
Chasing echoes in a whimsical dream.
Join this race, and take a seat,
In whimsical moments, life's sweet treat.

Curled Pathways of Reflection

Curled corners hide surprises tight,
Thoughts creep out, a hilarious sight.
Reflecting shadows, giggles peek,
In corners where the walls all speak.

A sock puppet shared a laugh,
While echoes plot a silly graph.
Curved reflections, nature's jest,
Life's a puzzle, and laughter's best.

Down winding paths of quirky cheer,
Thoughts will dance without a fear.
Bouncing off the walls they go,
Twisting, turning, in a show.

Join me down this wacky lane,
Where silly thoughts break every chain.
In every curl, a laugh to find,
In these paths of the wandering mind.

The Dance of Thoughts on a String

Thoughts like marionettes, they prance,
Tangled up in a silly dance.
One starts to twirl, then trips on a shoe,
While laughter erupts, as friends join too.

A jester's hat, a thought's disguise,
One catches a feather, oh what a surprise!
With ribbons of color, we spin and we sway,
Each moment a giggle, in bright array.

When a serious thought attempts to join,
It slips on a banana, oh what a groin!
As wisdom winks from the corners of eyes,
In this playful tangle, where humor lies.

So let's hold the string, and guide the mirth,
In the folly of thoughts, we find our worth.
With each little quirk, our minds take flight,
In the dance of our thoughts, we find pure delight.

Fragments of Time in Fragile Light

Time skips like stones on a glittering lake,
Each splash a giggle, a joke we can make.
Seconds drift by on a bubble of air,
Tickling our fancies, without a care.

A moment is lost in the folds of our minds,
While laughter erupts as the clock unwinds.
Fractal reflections, like shards of a dream,
In light, they flicker, a whimsical beam.

Juggling the present, we toss it up high,
As past and future take turns to fly.
A pie in the face, as time trips and spills,
We laugh at the chaos, replete with thrills.

In fragile light, each second a jest,
With giggles and gaffes, we give it our best.
We gather these fragments, like jewels they gleam,
A kaleidoscope of laughter, the heart's gentle beam.

Sway of Reflections on Tranquil Waters

The pond holds dreams that bubble and swirl,
Reflections of giggles in each little twirl.
A frog serenades in a goofy croon,
While fish dance below to a whimsical tune.

Ripples of chuckles cascade through the air,
Reflecting our joys, we float without care.
Each wave brings a quip, like a splash on our face,
In the laughter of water, we find our place.

Skimming a stone, we make wishes aloud,
They bounce off the surface, a playful crowd.
With quirks and with laughter, our spirits entwined,
We play in the ripples, leaving worries behind.

In the sway of reflections, we find our delight,
As shadows become laughter that dances in light.
In this tranquil moment, so silly and free,
We swim through our thoughts, just you and me.

Illumined Darkness in Inner Spaces

In the shadows that tickle our curious hearts,
Laughter ignites like a spark in the dark.
Thoughts whirl in circles, like fireflies do,
As they flicker and dance, bringing joy anew.

A treasure chest holds all the giggles and glee,
With silly surprises waiting just for thee.
In corners of quiet where nonsense can bloom,
We chuckle at echoes that brighten the room.

Whispers of whimsy float high on the breeze,
As we delve into humor with effortless ease.
These buried delights, like candy at night,
Illuminate inner spaces, a soft, glowing light.

So, let's dive into darkness, with mirth in our grip,
In the depths of our minds, take a joyful trip.
For in every dark corner, let laughter arise,
In the glow of our giggles, our spirit flies.

The Dance of Ideas

In a room where ideas spin,
A sock found its way, wearing a grin.
One thought tangoed with a chair,
While a spoon sighed, 'Why am I here?'

The cat joined in, a fuzzy delight,
Chasing shadows in the dim light.
Banana peels became a slide,
As giggles erupted, joy multiplied.

A random thought jumped on the bed,
Said, "Have you noticed the jellyfish spread?"
Laughter echoed through the air,
As ideas danced without a care.

So join the jive, it's quite the show,
When minds get lively, watch them flow.
A disco ball made of cheese,
In the land of musings, all is a tease.

Shadows of Reflection

In mirrors where thoughts twist and twirl,
A reflection winked, started to swirl.
It whispered secrets, then lost its grip,
As the lamp giggled, 'What's this trip?'

Thoughts floated like balloons in bloom,
Getting stuck under the couch like gloom.
A hat said, 'Today I'll lead the way!'
As they hopped around in a curious play.

The wall cracked jokes, a real smart fella,
While a stubborn chair became a challenger.
In a world where echoes love to tease,
Reflections bounce around with ease.

One thought tangled in spaghetti strands,
And declared, "I just need some hands!"
Giggles erupted from floor to wall,
As shadows of laughter answered the call.

Fleeting Fragments of Dreams

In dreams where bits and pieces collide,
A rubber duck took a joyous ride.
It quacked a tune that made folks smile,
As it floated on clouds for a while.

A dream fragment peeked from behind the door,
Said, "Let's dance on the kitchen floor!"
With a spatula leading, doing the twist,
Those fleeting thoughts, hard to resist.

The clock chimed in, 'What time is it now?'
As the sofa said, 'You'll never know how!'
A sock puppet told stories so grand,
That even the toaster couldn't withstand.

So catch those snippets before they flee,
Each quirky thought is truly free.
Laughter is a dream's best friend,
In fragments of joy, let's pretend!

Paths of Imagination

On paths where daydreams play and roam,
A squirrel in a cape claimed it's home.
With acorns for wheels, it zoomed on by,
Making up worlds where marshmallows fly.

A puddle became a portal of cheer,
Where flip-flops danced without any fear.
Imagined elephants in clown attire,
Performed on stage, igniting a fire.

Thoughts took a bus, made of candy canes,
Stopping by clouds, avoiding drains.
The stars held hands, as they giggled bright,
Creating constellations just for the night.

In this land where we wander and muse,
Every step's a chance for quirky cues.
With laughter as fuel and whimsy in sight,
Paths of the fanciful shine ever bright.

Spirals of Wonder and Enigma

In a world so round, I lost my shoe,
Time ticked sideways, how odd but true.
A squirrel warned me of a purse's might,
While shadows giggled, hiding from light.

My coffee brewed a plan to flee,
It whispered sweet nothings, just to me.
A new invention, a hat for my pen,
That pens could wear hats? My brain said, "When?"

A dance of ideas, like socks in the dryer,
They're twirling, they're spinning - a chaotic choir.
I laughed as I jiggled, with thoughts out of place,
Chasing a notion that wears a cat's face!

Oh, the wonders that wait in a foggy old chair,
With gumballs conversing, without a care.
How high can we fly with a shoe on one foot?
That daring dilemma! Oh, what a hoot!

Entangled Moments of Clarity

Walnuts dancing in an orchard so bright,
A hedgehog explained the joy of flight.
He claimed he could soar if only he'd try,
While birds rolled their eyes, way up in the sky.

Jellybeans giggled at my tangled hair,
Said, "Your thoughts are like bubbles! What a fair!"
I pondered a world where ideas come free,
And dances are started by mischievous glee.

A sock puppet argued with a spoon on the floor,
About who was destined to explore and soar.
Their banter was witty, perplexing yet fun,
As light danced around like a day in the sun.

In a pot of ideas, I stirred with delight,
Causing laughter to bloom, painting all in bright.
With a tickle of whimsy, confusion just fades,
Leaving chocolate rivers and marshmallow glades.

Twisting Streams of Awareness

Banana peels slipping on thoughts like a breeze,
Emotions that giggle, since doubt likes to tease.
I tripped on a dream wearing mismatched shoes,
How curious it felt, like dancing with blues.

A bumblebee buzzed about thinking it's cool,
Debating the merits of dropouts from school.
'Why not just wing it?' it whispered with pride,
While daisies around sparkled, eyes open wide.

Jellyfish pondering about life underwater,
All elegance lost when they bumped at the starter.
"Do thoughts have a form?" asked a starfish in jest,
With laughter echoing throughout this mad quest!

As shadows and light chase the day on a spree,
A tumble of giggles rounds out my day's glee.
In a whirl of bright colors, ideas take flight,
Spinning new stories from morning till night.

Blossoming Ideas in the Mist

In the garden of chatter where whispers grow tall,
A rabbit recited a nonsense-filled call.
"Do ducks wear capes?" was his quirky debate,
As clouds formed a chorus; they echoed, "Just wait!"

A pickle spied shadows where thoughts like to play,
Creating a tango beneath the sun's ray.
Each vine intertwined with a chuckle and snort,
Inventing a party where all could cavort!

Frisbees of wonder soared over the hill,
While crickets composed a symphony still.
A balloon filled with giggles drifted by chance,
Inviting each insect to join in the dance!

With ideas a-bloom, like flowers in spring,
I chuckled at ponderings, life's odd little fling.
For in each silly moment, a treasure appears,
In each tangled laughter, new visions endears.

Fragile Vines of Insight

In the garden of ideas, thoughts do twirl,
Like cats in a race, chasing every swirl.
A notion floats by, oh what a sight,
I grab it like candy, in sweet, silly delight.

A giggle of wisdom, sprouting with glee,
Tangled up laughter, just let it be.
The flowers are chuckling, the bees are so bold,
They buzz about secrets just waiting to be told.

With each twist and turn, my mind does dance,
Frolicking freely, in a thought-filled trance.
That one little whisper, where'd it run to?
Ah! Lost in the maze of my own wild brew.

So here in this patch of whimsical dreams,
I pluck the ripe moments, or so it seems.
A tip of the hat to the nonsense I seek,
For insight sometimes prefers. . . fun's the best peak!

Serpentine Paths of Belief

Down winding roads where silliness reigns,
I navigate thoughts like comical trains.
Beliefs are like rubber bands, stretching so wide,
Bouncing back quickly, with humor as guide.

Each curve is a chuckle, each twist a delight,
I tumble through notions, oh what a sight!
They spiral and swoop in the depths of my mind,
Unraveling kernels, oddly intertwined.

Up in the trees, convictions take flight,
A parrot of doubt squawks, but can't get it right.
I giggle through pathways, a jester's parade,
Where wisdom's wiggly and seldom delayed.

So let's cheer to the paths that lead us astray,
With laughter as compass, we'll dance and we'll sway.
In the forest of thought, wild and unkept,
We find our own truth, in the laughs we've leapt.

Flickers of Light in the Quiet

In whispers where shadows softly collide,
A flicker of nonsense leaps out to reside.
It dances on air with a twinkle and spin,
The silence erupts with a cheeky grin.

Oh, how they wiggle, these thoughts in the dark,
Each flash is a quirk, each spark a remark.
The quiet can burst with a giggle so sweet,
As laughter becomes the most dangerous treat.

Quietude shuffles, tiptoes with flair,
Illuminating minds with a ticklish care.
Bubbles of joy in an otherwise hush,
A reminder that giggles can always rush.

So when thoughts sit still like a cat on a bed,
Throw in a comet to brighten your head.
For just like a spark that can't help but ignite,
In moments of stillness, we dance with our light!

Braided Streams of Consciousness

In streams that entwine like a comical tale,
Thoughts crisscross and bubble like soda's sweet sail.
Each twist is a giggle, each turn is a jest,
Winding together, they're simply the best.

A fish swims upstream, but I float with the tide,
Chasing the humor that bubbles inside.
Wet and wild laughter, I let it all flow,
Where consciousness tangles, what a fun show!

Imaginations whirl in a soft, silly pool,
Plucking at ideas, I find them quite cool.
A splash here, a dash there, my mind will collide,
With whimsy and wonder as life's joyful guide.

So as currents do shift, and thoughts swirl about,
I'll chase every giggle, and banish the doubt.
For in this great river of laughter and dreams,
The braided streams of my mind are bursting at seams!

The Fabric of Reverie

In a world where socks get lost,
Thoughts do pirouettes at a cost.
A dance of ideas, both silly and spry,
Like a cat in a hat, oh my, oh my!

Napkins flutter in culinary dreams,
Sauces whisper in giggling streams.
Imagined feasts where no one gets fat,
While spoons conspire to wear a top hat.

We weave the fabric with threads of our mind,
The quirkiest bits we can possibly find.
Yarn balls of chaos, assorted and bright,
Knitting up laughter, both day and night.

So let's pluck thoughts like ripe, juicy fruit,
And shuffle our dreams in mismatched boots.
In this realm, so zany, we feel quite alive,
With each stitch of whimsy, we laugh and thrive.

Interlaced Whispers of Wonder

Whispers tickle like feathers in flight,
Curly cues chase the fading daylight.
Thoughts bounce around like popcorn on heat,
In the microwave of what's funny and sweet.

Giggling clouds do their fluffy ballet,
While dreaming of tacos that dance and sway.
Puns take a spin on a merry-go-round,
Taste buds chortle at flavors profound.

Bubbles of laughter, they flute and they leap,
Over dreams where thoughts take a crazy sweep.
Delicate fancies, like spiders in lace,
Spin webs of jest in a wild, warm embrace.

Each idea prances, a jester on stage,
Filling our hearts with a whimsical rage.
As rainbows poke fun with their vivid display,
We giggle at life—a bright cabaret.

Cascading Thoughts Like Vines

Thoughts cascade like ivy, all tangled and bright,
Climbing walls of my mind in the moon's soft light.
They stretch out their tendrils, amusing the breeze,
Wrapping giggles and snickers as easy as peas.

Spaghetti surprises dance on a plate,
As thoughts stretch like noodles, oh isn't that great?
Fuzzy ideas stick to the tip of my nose,
While pondering why socks are in such odd clothes.

Babbling brooks of laughter bubble and flow,
Mirth mingles with whispers, 'tis quite the show.
Each twist of a thought is a knot in the air,
Filled with mischief, like kittens that dare.

In gardens of humor, we frolic and play,
Where nonsense and joy twine merrily away.
So gather your giggles, let's throw them about,
In the jungles of whimsy, let's dance and shout!

Seeds of Illumination

Planting ideas in laughter's warm soil,
Sprouting joy like a mischievous foil.
Biting into snacks where the laughter's gone wild,
Discussing the merits of a taco-styled child.

Jellybeans grow from the silliest dreams,
Sailing on wishes like whimsical beams.
The fruit of our thoughts, ripe with delight,
Jumps in to play in the dead of the night.

In gardens of giggles, we scatter our seeds,
Watering nonsense with whimsical deeds.
Fertilized by chuckles, they blossom and bloom,
In the patch of our minds, there's always more room.

So let's sow a harvest of bright, crazy lore,
Dig deep with our rakes and giggle some more.
With each joyful seed, let forgetful frowns fade,
As sprouts of illumination dance in parade.

Colliding Realities in Subtle Vibrance

In the kitchen, a cat wore a hat,
While my toaster said, 'What's up with that?'
A spoon did the cha-cha with a fork,
As the fridge chimed in with a cheesy cork.

Peppers danced wild on the cutting board,
Mushrooms wiggled, it's kitchen accord.
The clock ticked slow, but the humor sped,
As my salad dreamed of a life well-fed.

Gravity, it seems, took a coffee break,
As carrots debated which one was fake.
When laughter erupted from a bowl of beans,
Even the napkins joined in the scenes.

Who knew the spatula had perfect moves?
While lettuce was lost in its silly grooves.
A symphony of chaos, all quite absurd,
Life's little moments, oh how they stirred!

Hazy Trails of Awareness

A squirrel on a skateboard took flight,
Chasing shadows in the park's golden light.
The trees whispered gossip, oh what a tease,
While I wondered if owls wear slippers with ease.

My thoughts meandered, like a creek on a stroll,
As clouds traded secrets, making the roll.
A grasshopper giggled just out of view,
Declare it a party, with bumbles and boo!

The daisies were plotting their great flowering scheme,
While ants dressed in tuxes prepared for a dream.
Laughter erupted as I chased the warm breeze,
With every odd moment, my mind found its keys.

Tangled reflections in a puddle so sly,
Should I leap through these thoughts—give it a try?
From giggles to snorts, then a chuckling wheeze,
Life spun in frames like a movie with cheese.

Petals Lifted by a Gentle Breeze

The flowers were gossiping quite out of turn,
With a bee buzzing loudly, they'd chatter and churn.
A daisy declared she was queen of the patch,
While tulips winked slyly, a colorful batch.

A butterfly tripped over its own silky wing,
And the vines sighed deeply at such silly things.
As petals took flight in a ballet of hues,
It felt like a show, complete with grand views.

Grass blades waved hello, in their verdant attire,
And the sun threw a smile, it's hardly a liar.
Of all the bouquets that bloomed in the spree,
You'd think this garden was shy of its glee.

When the breeze came to tease, oh, what a sight,
Petals did pirouettes like stars in the night.
With laughter and sparkles twirling with ease,
Each moment's a dance, carried soft by the breeze.

Strands of Feeling in the Cosmic Web

A spaghetti monster looked down from above,
With meatballs for planets, oh what a love!
The stars blinked brightly, like eyes in a dance,
While noodle galaxies took a night-time romance.

Meanwhile, on Earth, a dog wore a cape,
Chasing shadows of squirrels, oh what a shape!
His thoughts twirled around, like confetti in air,
As he barked at the moon with a jubilant flair.

The sun chuckled loudly at its own shining,
Making rays of laughter, all brightly aligning.
As theories of noodle unspooled in delight,
Even the cosmos giggled into the night.

Each strand of feeling, a puppet on strings,
Frolicking along with the joy that it brings.
In the web of existence, where whimsy does flow,
Life's playful absurdity is all that we know.

Driftwood Thoughts Along the River

I tossed my dreams like driftwood,
They floated by with odd intent.
A fish nibbled on my good mood,
While the current laughed and bent.

Bright ideas bobbed, quite silly,
Swirling round in laughter's stream.
A turtle thought it was all frilly,
As I chased a half-formed dream.

The river's whispers held such glee,
In a dance of quirky delight.
Beckoning thoughts to swim with me,
Underneath the stars so bright.

But when I tried to catch a plan,
It slipped away with a cheeky grin.
Life's just a game of hide and scan,
Where winning means you never win.

The Weight of Lost Endeavors

I weighed my hopes like hefty bricks,
They tumbled down, a clumsy stack.
Each one unveiled its funny tricks,
As plans went off the beaten track.

Up in the air, the ideas flew,
Like kites caught up in winter's gust.
They tangled up with all that's blue,
Leaving me chuckling, 'what a bust!'

On Monday's list, a grand pursuit,
By Friday's noon, they drifted east.\nNow all that's left's an elephant suit,
That makes me giggle, at the least.

So here's to dreams that went askew,
A circus of sorts in my head.
Juggling thoughts that slipped right through,
And landing softly, instead of dead.

Shimmering Lumens in the Mind's Cavern

In the cavern of my mind, I see,
Glowing ideas dance like fireflies.
They flicker whimsically, so free,
Beaming thoughts with zany highs.

One bounces off a stalactite,
While another drapes its light in jest.
They mock my effort, but that's all right,
I revel in their chaotic fest.

My brain's a disco ball at night,
Reflecting laughter in every beam.
I stumble through this glowing sight,
Chasing shadows, chasing a dream.

Bright comets zoom past my ear,
Comedic echoes ring the round.
With every giggle, thoughts appear,
As lumens swirl and spin around.

Unfurling Scrolls of Possibility

I found a scroll beneath my bed,
It promised fortunes, oh so grand.
But every word was full of lead,
And made me laugh, as I now stand.

It unfurled tales so far-fetched,
Of carrots that could dance and sing.
While in my heart, joy was etched,
In playful dreams, I felt the zing.

I scribbled notes in colored ink,
On kitchen curtains, on the wall.
Each idea made me stop and think,
And burst out laughing through it all.

The scrolls may promise much delight,
But end up waltzing out of line.
What fun, to dream and take flight,
In the theater of the mind's design.

Swaying Leaves of Imagination

In the garden of ideas, trees grow wide,
Silly thoughts flutter like butterflies inside.
A squirrel in a hat tells tales of the day,
As twirls of giggles dance in playful sway.

Clouds wear their whiskers, as if in disguise,
Juggling bright planets, oh what a surprise!
A toad sings in chorus, a croakful delight,
While shadows throw punches in the glow of light.

Labyrinthine Echoes in Silence

Echoes of answer tramp through my mind,
Each twist and turn leads to laughter aligned.
An owl with a monocle reads a lost page,
While the mice host debates on what cheese is sage.

Tickling the corners of thoughts in a spiral,
The whispers of nonsense engage in a trial.
With serious faces, they argue and jest,
Claiming the oddest of thoughts is the best.

Merging Currents of Emotion

Waves of whimsy crash upon the shore,
Where emotions jumble and twirl even more.
A jellyfish in a tuxedo floats neat,
While crabs clap their claws to a jazzy beat.

Rainbows collide in a sprightly parade,
Each color a punchline, a joke long delayed.
With sprinkles of giggles like confetti in air,
The sea bubbles over with playful despair.

Fleeting Moments in the Twilight

Twilight flutters like a shy little sprite,
Painting the world in a whimsical light.
A dog in pajamas chases stars that tease,
While crickets play harps under swaying trees.

Laughter drips slowly like honey in time,
As shadows pirouette, a playful rhyme.
With each blink of dusk, the moments escape,
Leaving footprints of giggles for dreams to reshape.

Branches of Contemplation

I once thought of a branch, quite small and spry,
Contemplating life, as it waved goodbye.
It danced in the breeze, with a flourish and spin,
Wondering where all the good nuts had been.

The squirrels chimed in, with laughter galore,
"You're overthinking, just settle the score!"
They jumped and they jived, with a cheer and a pout,
As the branch pondered who'd keep its thoughts out.

So up it stretched forth, into the big sky,
Imagining clouds as marshmallows up high.
But the more that it thought, the more it was stuck,
It waved down at squirrels; they just said, "Good luck!"

At last, it let go, of its worrisome fret,
To summon the joy of a little duet.
With sighs of relief, it finally twirled,
A branch fully free, from the weight of the world.

The Tapestry of Insight

In a room full of fabric, insights did weave,
A tapestry chuckled, with tales to believe.
"What if I stitched a cat wearing a hat?"
It pondered along, as a needle grew fat.

It painted the world, scene by odd scene,
A dog in a tux, on a bike, looking keen.
With a flick of its thread, it tacked on a dance,
A llama in boots, what a wild circumstance!

The colors danced brightly, with laughter and flair,
Double-checking stitches, the fabric did care.
"Am I too over the top, a tad out of line?"
"No worries!" said the yarn, "It's a whimsical sign!"

So it sewed through the night, till the morning light gleamed,
Creating a fabric of thoughts that all dreamed.
And as folks peered in, giving gasps of delight,
They laughed at the stories, all stitched up just right.

Spirals of Perception

In a spiral of curls, a rabbit did say,
"Perception is funny; it leads me astray!"
I thought I'd found carrots, so sweet and so bright,
But ended up gnawing on a shoe in the night.

The more that I twisted, the less I could see,
What thoughts were truly, just me being me.
"Is that a new path, or a word I forgot?"
Spirals of distance, in thinking, a lot!

While chasing my tail, I found wisdom, for sure,
In the crazy old loops, I could feel quite secure.
So I hopped with delight, in circles galore,
Rediscovering the things that I'd thought were a bore.

And now I embrace, every twist that I find,
With a laugh and a wiggle, I don't mind the grind.
For what seems convoluted may just be a way,
Of reminding us all, that we're having a play!

Rooted in Reverie

A tree deeply rooted, with thoughts down below,
Whispered to grass blades, as they danced to and fro.
"Do you think about growing? Or is that too deep?"
The grass giggled back, "I just want some sleep!"

The branches then chuckled, or rustled, who knows?
"Deeper thoughts, fine, but oh how it grows!"
They mused about leaves that may fall with the breeze,
And considered their past, like grand memories.

A squirrel popped up from his slumbering dream,
"I heard all your talk, it's not what it seems!"
With a flick of his tail, he declared with a grin,
"Sometimes the depths hide a giggle within!"

So together they laughed, in a light-hearted stew,
Rooted in whimsy, oh, who knew it was true?
That thoughts don't have to be heavy and sore,
They can spark joy and delight; who could ask for more?

Lifted Echoes from the Deep

In the ocean of my mind, I float,
Chasing bubbles, giggling like a goat.
Thoughts pop up, like corks on the sea,
Each one whispers silly things to me.

A jellyfish with a very big smile,
Dances around, oh, what a style!
Nautilus chuckles, shell on his back,
Says, "Your worries? Just a big snack!"

Mermaids sing tunes of silly delight,
While seaweed serves as disco light.
With octopus arms so clumsy and weird,
They juggle my worries—oh, how they jeered!

Back to the surface with a splash and a wink,
Wondering what I just forgot to think.
But laughter echoes through the deep,
A treasure found, I'll always keep.

Gossamer Threads of Emotion

A spider spins tales, oh so fine,
In a web of giggles, each strand divine.
Tickles from laughter float through the air,
As butterflies dance without a care.

Silken whispers in a ticklish breeze,
Thoughts flutter like leaves from the trees.
A squirrel chimes in with acorn delight,
While making up rhymes that feel just right.

Colors burst forth like paint in a splash,
Each hue a chuckle, bright and brash.
Wrapped in a hug of sheer playfulness,
I chase all the quirks I never guess.

As evening sets in, with stars all aglitter,
I tickle my brain, expecting it to twitter.
A funny parade begins in my chest,
In the tapestry woven, I'm surely blessed.

Murmurs in the Hall of Mind

In the hall of thoughts, echoes abound,
Clumsy ideas bounce off the ground.
A banana peel slips with a loud screech,
Which makes healthy eating seem out of reach.

Sconces of laughter light up the way,
As socks start to dance, come out to play.
A grandfather clock ticks in a twist,
Chimes in with giggles that can't be missed.

A frog croaks a joke, so ribbiting true,
While pondering life in a tutu and shoe.
Doors creak wide, is that what I hear?
A rabble of musings, spreading good cheer!

With each step I take, the floors softly groan,
Whispering secrets from the wacky unknown.
In this merry hall of whimsy and jest,
Every murmured thought feels like a party guest.

Silken Strands of Contemplation

On threads of silk, my musings sway,
Like kittens at play on a sunny day.
A caterpillar giggles, rolling about,
Wonders what life's truly about.

Clouds make faces, drifting slowly high,
While thoughts of world peace seem shy to fly.
A worm in a tux says, "I'll lead the dance!"
Twisting through soil, hoping for a chance.

A rubber duck floats on a ponderous pond,
Quacking profound things, of which I'm quite fond.
Each ripple a chuckle, sleek and serene,
In the landscape of dreams where giggles convene.

I drift in and out, like a kite on a breeze,
Chasing nonsense while doing as I please.
In this soft cocoon of whimsical ways,
Every thought a delight, brightening my days.

Subtle Currents of Yearning

In the fridge, I see my dreams,
A pizza slice lost, or so it seems.
With every chomp, my hopes revive,
Can cheese really keep desires alive?

Thoughts wander like socks in the dryer,
Each spin stirring up a quiet fire.
I chase the cat, who's plotting schemes,
While pondering what's missing from my dreams.

The clock ticks loud as I take a sip,
Of coffee that's fierce, like a pirate's trip.
My aspirations blend with cream and sweet,
A recipe for something quite unique.

Yet in a blink, those visions fly,
As a bee buzzes in, oh my, oh my!
But what was I after? I forgot the prize,
Maybe it's time for a slice of pie!

Interwoven Dreams in the Solstice

Beneath the sun, I dream of shade,
A hammock sways, my plans well laid.
I thought of mangoes, but found a rock,
In my daydreams, it's fruit that I mock.

The solstice sun shines like a light bulb,
In my tangled thoughts, it starts to curve.
A picnic planned, but who would come?
Last time it rained, we huddled in a drum.

My mind's a circus, with clowns and more,
Juggling worries and dreams galore.
A hotdog rolls dreams in mustard bright,
Oh, the great escape in the summer night.

Twinkle lights strung, for a party to host,
But why are my guests just thoughts and toast?
With laughter echoing under the trees,
I toast to dreams, and an endless breeze!

The Fabric of Musing

Knit one, purl two, my thoughts entwined,
In this yarn of life, what will I find?
A sweater of wondering, with pockets deep,
Hiding the secrets that make me weep.

Patterns emerge, a stitch here and there,
Frogging my doubts without a care.
Each row a journey, each loop, a grin,
What will I wear once this day begins?

With needles clicking, the chatter flows,
Of weekend plans and kitchen woes.
My socks have holes; should I knit them new?
Or maybe just wear them with a shoe or two?

The fabric of thought, it pulls and tugs,
Like a cat attacking those thoughtful hugs.
But weaving humor into my thread,
Keeps the laughter alive instead!

Orbiting Thoughts in the Stillness

In the quiet of night, ideas spin,
Like planets colliding or a dance grin.
A comet of laughter zooms by my bed,
Tickling my senses, it's filling my head.

The stars above wink, what do they know?
While I try to catch thoughts, like a show.
They orbit my mind, circling 'round,
Waiting for stardust to make them profound.

A black hole of worries looms near,
But I throw in giggles; they disappear.
Asteroids of chaos hit the ground,
Yet space is so vast, I'm still safe and sound.

Each thought a satellite, spinning in place,
As I float in this cosmic embrace.
With humor as fuel, I glide through the night,
Orbiting dreams that feel just right.

www.ingramcontent.com/pod-product-compliance
Lightning Source LLC
Chambersburg PA
CBHW072223070526
44585CB00015B/1465